MW00803459

The Duties and Responsibilities of
the Secretary of Homeland Security

David C. Ruffin

The Rosen Publishing Group's
PowerKids Press™
New York

Dedicated to my nieces and nephews

Published in 2005 by The Rosen Publishing Group, Inc.
29 East 21st Street, New York, NY 10010

First Edition

Editor: Frances E. Ruffin
Book Design: Albert B. Hanner
Photo Researcher: Sherri Liberman

Photo Credits: Cover (left, and right), pp. 4, 7, 11 (top), 12 (top), 16 (top and bottom), 19 (top), 20 (bottom), 23, 24 (bottom) © AP/Wide World Photo; p. 8 Courtesy US Secret Service Archives; pp. 11 (bottom), 27 © Hulton/Archive/Getty Images; p. 12 (bottom) © Bruce Chambers/Orange County Register/Corbis; p. 15 US Coast Guard Photo by PA3 Mike Hvozda; p. 19 (bottom) © Ron Sachs/Corbis; p. 20 (top) © Rob Varela/Ventura County Star/Corbis; p. 24 © Najlah Feanny/Corbis.

Library of Congress Cataloging-in-Publication Data

Ruffin, David C.
  The duties and responsibilities of the Secretary of Homeland Security / David C. Ruffin.— 1st ed.
      p. cm. — (Your government in action)
  Includes index.
  ISBN 1-4042-2693-1 (lib. bdg.)
  1. United States. Dept. of Homeland Security-Juvenile literature. 2. Terrorism—United States—Prevention—Juvenile literature. 3. National security—United States—Juvenile literature. I. Title.

  HV6432.4.R84 2005
  363.3'0973—dc22
                                        2004001127

Manufactured in the United States of America

Contents

A National Tragedy

On the morning of September 11, 2001, a group of terrorists attacked the two World Trade Center buildings in New York City. Terrorists are people who use **violence** to scare people. They flew airplanes full of passengers into the towers. The buildings caught fire, and soon they fell to the ground. Thousands of people were killed. Terrorists flew a third plane into the Pentagon. The Pentagon is the central office of the U.S. Armed Forces, located near Washington, D.C. After this national **tragedy**, America's leaders did not want anything like it to happen again. America's leaders decided to form a new governmental **agency** to protect the country from terrorist attacks. Formed in 2001, the agency was called the Office of Homeland Security. That agency would grow to become the Department of Homeland Security.

◀ *This image shows the remains of the World Trade Center buildings after the attack. About 3,000 people died in the national tragedy on September 11, 2001.*

The Newest Secretary

U.S. Congress formed the Department of Homeland Security in 2002. In January 2003, President George W. Bush appointed Tom Ridge as the first secretary of the department. The secretary's main job is to **defend** the United States from terrorist attacks. Before he became secretary, Tom Ridge was the governor of Pennsylvania from 1995 to 2001. He was also a member of the U.S. House of Representatives from 1982 to 1994. The House is a part of Congress, which makes laws for America. Tom Ridge fought in the Vietnam War (1965–1973) and was given a **medal** for bravery. The secretary of homeland security position is the newest addition to the cabinet of the U.S. president. The cabinet is made up of people who are the most important advisers to the president. These advisers also run the largest agencies in the U.S. government.

Tom Ridge is sworn in as secretary of the Department of Homeland Security. The secretary's job is to protect American citizens from attacks that come from within the United States.

Members of the U.S. Secret Service are always with the president when he is in public. The people in the Secret Service work hard to keep the president, the vice president, and others safe.

One Department from Many Agencies

The 180,000 governmental **employees** in the Department of Homeland Security help the secretary to protect American people. They work to protect people from attacks made from within the United States. Most of the agencies that are part of the department have existed for a long time. For example, the Secret Service was formed in 1865 and has protected the U.S. president since 1894. The U.S. Coast Guard has guarded our shores for more than 200 years.

Twenty-two governmental agencies were brought into one department so that protecting American citizens could be better organized. The Department of Homeland Security is different from the Department of Defense. The Department of Defense is in charge of the Army, Navy, Air Force, and Marines. It protects the United States from attacks or **threats** from outside the country.

Protecting U.S. Borders

The biggest agency of the Department of Homeland Security is the Directorate of Border and **Transportation** Security (BTS). BTS combines several organizations that already existed. They took over the parts of the Immigration and Naturalization Service (INS) that guard against people coming illegally into the United States. One of these parts is the Border Patrol, which works to stop people from crossing borders illegally in ways like hiding in trucks. BTS also took over the U.S. **Customs** Service, which looks out for **dangerous** things, such as **explosives** and certain chemicals, entering the country. The Animal and Plant Health **Inspection** Service watches for animals or plants that have diseases, or illnesses, that could kill or harm animals and people. Mad cow disease is one such illness. The Transportation Security Administration protects America's transportation systems so people can travel safely.

◀ Members of the Border Patrol guard the International Bridge in Buffalo, New York. This bridge lies on the border between the United States and Canada and could be attacked by terrorists.

◀ Men from the U.S. Customs Service and the U.S. Coast Guard check a shipment of drugs that was being brought illegally into the country.

The Transportation Security Administration and the Customs and Border Protection (CBP) Agency are in charge of security at airports and seaports. Specially trained dogs are used to help find harmful or illegal products that are being brought into the country.

Airport security checks cars as they enter the airport. These security checkpoints are just one way the Department of Homeland Security keeps America safe.

Watching for Dangerous People

The most important task of BTS is to watch for harmful people entering the country. This is the job of Customs and Border Protection (CBP), which is the agency that houses the Border Patrol and Customs Service. Each year more than 330 million people come into the United States who are not American citizens. CBP watches the 5,525-mile (8,892-km) border that America shares with Canada and the 1,989-mile (3,201-km) border that America shares with Mexico. CBP and the Transportation Security Administration watch airports and seaports. These agencies pay attention to who enters America, but they do not want to keep people from visiting who do not mean any harm. The secretary of homeland security does not want to stop goods from entering or leaving the country. The job of the secretary and the agencies he or she oversees is to make sure Americans are safe.

Guarding Our Coasts

The secretary of homeland security now oversees the U.S. Coast Guard, which was created by Congress in 1789. Using ships, planes, and helicopters, the Coast Guard has the job of guarding America's 95,000 miles (152,888 km) of shoreline. This includes the Atlantic Coast, the Pacific Coast, the Caribbean Sea, the Gulf of Mexico, and the Great Lakes. The Coast Guard makes sure that ships can bring goods into and out of the United States safely. Another job of the Coast Guard is to stop **smugglers** from bringing weapons, **illegal aliens**, and dangerous drugs like cocaine into the United States. In 2002, the Coast Guard captured $3.9 billion worth of cocaine from smugglers.

A Coast Guard boat patrols New York City Harbor with a New York Police Department boat. National and local agencies work together as part of Operation Liberty Shield. This is the Department of Homeland Security's plan to make sure ports and waterways are safe.

Val Klump, director of the Center for Water Security, is shown giving a tour of the center in Milwaukee, Wisconsin, in 2003. The scientists at this center work to keep drinking water safe from terrorists.

The Indian Point power plants in Buchanan, New York, create much of the electricity for the area. Without electricity, our telephones and computers would not work and we would have no lights or television.

Safeguarding Our Food, Water, and Electricity

The secretary of homeland security helps to guard the nation's **critical infrastructure**. The critical infrastructure is made up of the many things that we need to continue our way of life. The infrastructure includes the water we drink and the food we get from farms. It includes the transportation systems we depend on, such as buses, trains, and subways. The electricity we use and our communications systems are other important parts of the critical infrastructure. Communication systems are things like the telephone or the radio by which people share news.

If terrorists attacked our infrastructure, they could make it hard for us to do the things we do every day. The secretary of homeland security sends teams to state and local governments to help figure out the dangers to the infrastructure and how to protect it.

Guarding Against Biological Attacks

The secretary of Homeland Security must guard against **biological attacks** by terrorists. Biological attacks might come in the form of illnesses such as smallpox and anthrax. These illnesses can kill millions of people, but they are hard to detect, or find. In October 2001, a terrorist sent envelopes of the anthrax **virus** in the form of a white powder to two senators' offices in Washington, D.C. Five people died.

The Department of Homeland Security's Lawrence Livermore National Laboratory in California works to prevent biological attacks. The scientists at the laboratory are creating ways to detect deadly viruses. They are also creating vaccines against them. Vaccines are shots that keep a person from getting sick.

18

◄ Hazardous-materials experts check for anthrax in Washington, D.C. Hazardous-materials experts are people who have a lot of knowledge in dealing with dangerous biological and chemical weapons.

◄ After the anthrax attack in 2001, people who handled mail wore masks and gloves to protect themselves.

Homeowners in southern California watch as a wildfire burns on a nearby hillside. About five thousand firefighters fought fires that covered more than 250,000 acres (101,171 ha).

A man saves his cat from the fast-moving floodwaters caused by a burst dam in West Des Moines, Iowa.

Floods, Fires, and Hurricanes

The secretary of homeland security is in charge of the Federal Emergency Management Agency (FEMA). FEMA helps people get through **disasters**. If there were another attack like the one on September 11, 2001, FEMA would help the victims. Not all tragedies that happen in the United States are caused by humans, however. The secretary of homeland security is also responsible for helping Americans who are victims of natural disasters, such as hurricanes, floods, wildfires, and winter storms. FEMA helps local governments prepare for emergencies. If a town is flooded or hit by a hurricane, FEMA helps the people who live there with food, shelter, medicine, and **evacuation** from dangerous areas. FEMA helps homebuilders and construction companies to create buildings that will last through disasters like hurricanes and **earthquakes**.

Getting Information to the People

Because of the attacks of September 11, 2001, the United States will always have to be ready for a terrorist attack. One of the most important jobs of the secretary of homeland security is to let the American people know when there is danger of an attack. This is done through the Directorate of Information Analysis and the Threat Advisory System. The level of danger is given a Threat Condition Color. The colors range from green at the lowest threat level to red at the highest. The directorate announces the Threat Condition Color on television, on the radio, and in the newspapers. People can make decisions about what they will do and where they will go based on the threat condition in a certain place.

Tom Ridge explains the Threat Advisory System for the first time. If the Threat Condition Color is green, the danger of a terrorist attack is at its lowest. The Threat Condition Color moves to blue, then yellow, orange, and red, as the danger of an attack increases.

New Yorkers are able to do their shopping for emergency supplies at a store called Safer America, which opened after the attacks of September 11, 2001. Here gas masks are shown.

These men rush to board up the windows on their building before a hurricane arrives. Boarding up windows can protect a building from the dangerous winds of a hurricane.

Educating the Public

In the case of a terrorist attack or a natural disaster, the Department of Homeland Security needs help from the public. Americans have to be educated to help themselves in a disaster. The department's Directorate of Emergency Preparedness and Response provides useful information to people on how to prepare for an emergency. The department wants to be sure that people can survive a disaster until the government is able to send help.

The Office for Domestic Preparedness (ODP) is part of the directorate. It is the main office responsible for preparing the United States for acts of terrorism. The ODP provides training, funds, and other support to help local governments prevent, plan for, and respond to acts of terrorism.

To prepare for an emergency, your family can put aside at least three days of food and water for each family member. The food should be ready to eat in case there is no electricity. Have a first-aid kit, a flashlight, and a radio that runs on batteries, as well as a sleeping bag or a warm blanket.

US-VISIT Program

US-VISIT is a program of the Department of Homeland Security that helps track visitors to the United States. Travelers needing special permission to enter the United States must have their photograph taken at the airport or seaport and leave two fingerprints. The fingerprints and the photo are stored in a computer to help immigration officers decide who is entering the United States legally. They can also match this information to data on special watchlists of dangerous people.

The secretary of homeland security believes that most people come to the United States for good reasons, such as business, education, or visiting relatives. The purpose of the US-VISIT program is to welcome visitors who come here for good reasons while also protecting Americans from terrorists. This is just another way the secretary of homeland security is working to keep America safe.

A customs and border protection officer uses the new US-VISIT program. The computer checks the photo and fingerprints of the person entering the country.

Secretaries of Homeland Security from 2001 to 2005

Tom Ridge, 2001–2005

Agencies That Formed the Department

These are some of the agencies that came from other departments in the federal government to make up the Department of Homeland Security:

- ▶ The Coast Guard was taken from the Department of Transportation.
- ▶ The Transportation Security Administration was taken from Department of Transportation.
- ▶ The U.S. Secret Service was taken from the Treasury Department.
- ▶ The U.S. Customs Service was taken from the Treasury Department.
- ▶ The Federal Law Enforcement Training Center was taken from the Treasury Department.
- ▶ Part of the Immigration and Naturalization Service was taken from the Justice Department.
- ▶ The Border Patrol was taken from the Justice Department.
- ▶ The Animal and Plant Health Inspection Service was taken from the Department of Agriculture.
- ▶ The Federal Protective Service was taken from the General Services Administration.
- ▶ The Federal Emergency Management Agency was an independent agency.

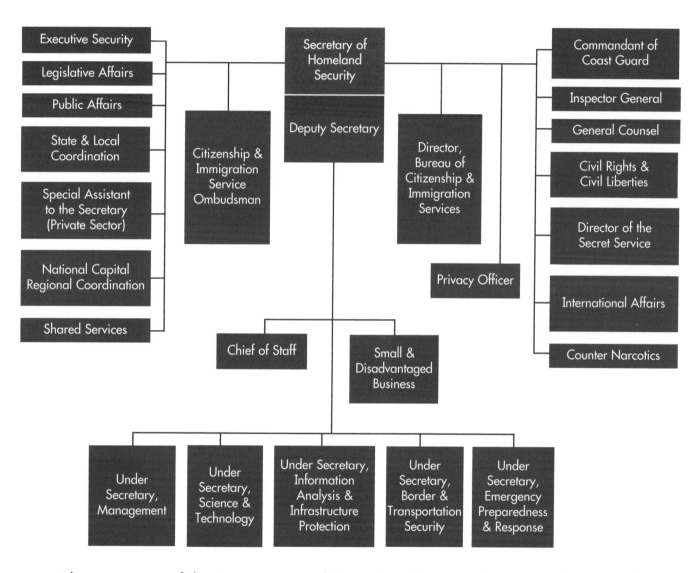

		Secretary of Homeland Security		

- Executive Security
- Legislative Affairs
- Public Affairs
- State & Local Coordination
- Special Assistant to the Secretary (Private Sector)
- National Capital Regional Coordination
- Shared Services

Citizenship & Immigration Service Ombudsman

Deputy Secretary

Director, Bureau of Citizenship & Immigration Services

Privacy Officer

- Commandant of Coast Guard
- Inspector General
- General Counsel
- Civil Rights & Civil Liberties
- Director of the Secret Service
- International Affairs
- Counter Narcotics

Chief of Staff

Small & Disadvantaged Business

Under Secretary, Management

Under Secretary, Science & Technology

Under Secretary, Information Analysis & Infrastructure Protection

Under Secretary, Border & Transportation Security

Under Secretary, Emergency Preparedness & Response

The secretary of the Department of Homeland Security has many duties and responsibilities. The thousands of people who assist the secretary work in the agencies of the department that are outlined in this chart.

Timeline

September 11, 2001	Terrorists attack the World Trade Center and the Pentagon.
September 20, 2001	President Bush announces the creation of the Office of Homeland Security and appoints Governor Tom Ridge as director.
October 26, 2001	President Bush signs the USA Patriot Act, which gives intelligence and law enforcement agencies new tools to use to fight terrorism.
March 12, 2002	President Bush establishes the Threat Advisory System, which measures and evaluates the threat and informs the public through a color-coded system.
May 14, 2002	President Bush signs the Border Security and Visa Entry Reform Act, which helps to secure U.S. borders.
November 25, 2002	President Bush signs the Homeland Security Act of 2002, which creates the Department of Homeland Security.
January 2003	Tom Ridge becomes secretary of Homeland Security.
March 18, 2003	Secretary Ridge announces Operation Liberty Shield, an effort to increase the security and preparedness of the United States in the event of a wide variety of terrorist attacks.
April 29, 2003	The Department of Homeland Security announces US-VISIT program for travelers.

Glossary

agency (AY-jen-see) A special department of the government.

biological attacks (by-uh-LAH-jih-kul uh-TAKS) Attacks made using living things.

critical infrastructure (KRIH-tih-kul IN-freh-struk-chur) The important things, such as electricity, telephones, and water, that allow us to live the way we do.

customs (KUS-tumz) A part of the government that collects taxes on goods entering or leaving the country.

dangerous (DAYN-jer-us) Able to cause harm.

defend (dih-FEND) To guard from harm.

disasters (dih-ZAS-terz) Events that cause suffering or loss.

earthquake (erth-KWAYK) A shaking of Earth's surface.

employees (im-ploy-EEZ) People who are paid to work for a person or a business.

evacuation (ih-va-kyuh-WAY-shun) The immediate leaving of an unsafe area.

explosives (ek-SPLOH-sivz) Things that can explode.

illegal aliens (ih-LEE-gul AY-lee-unz) People from another country who are in a place unlawfully.

inspection (in-SPEK-shun) The act of checking over closely.

medal (MEH-dul) A small, round piece of metal that is given as a prize.

smugglers (SMUH-glurz) People who sneak things in and out of a country.

threats (THRETS) People or things that may be harmful.

tragedy (TRA-jeh-dee) A very sad event.

transportation (tranz-per-TAY-shun) A way of traveling from one place to another.

violence (VY-lens) Strong force used to cause harm.

virus (VY-rus) Something tiny that causes an illness.

Index

Web Sites

Due to the changing nature of Internet links, PowerKids Press has developed an online list of Web sites related to the subject of this book. This site is updated regularly. Please use this link to access the list:
www.powerkidslinks.com/yga/drshs/